On to the next job!

T0321841

Written by M J Hooton

Illustrated by Parwinder Singh

Collins

Param and Petra are paramedics.

3

They rush to Grandad Peng.

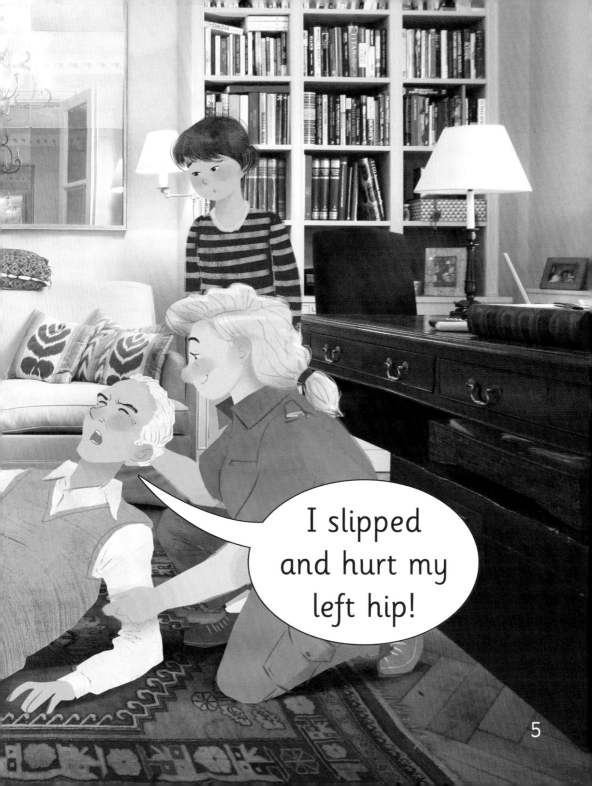

5

The ramp lifts Grandad Peng up.

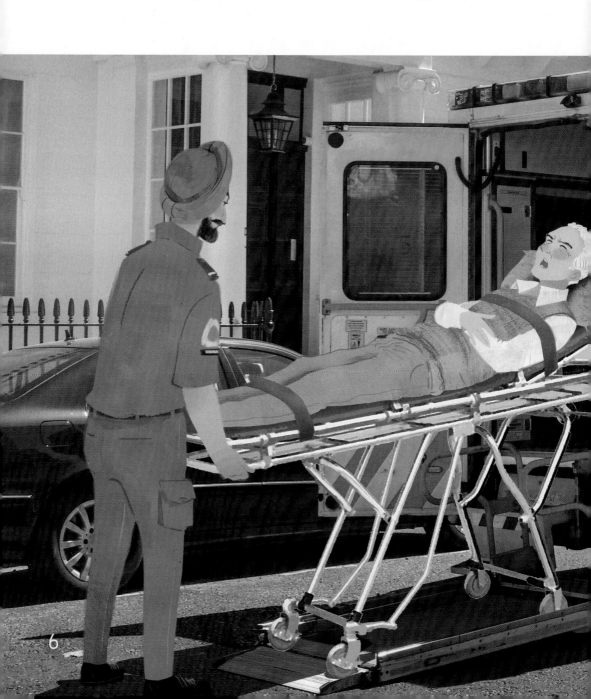

They transport him to be seen
by the medics.

On to the next job! Param turns on the flashing lights and off they go.

Fran was up her ladder picking plums when she crashed down, hurting her leg.

Petra straps a splint onto Fran's hurt leg to keep it still on the trip.

10

The paramedics are off in a flash to get Fran checked.

Ring ring! Param must sprint.
His little one will be born soon!

Jobs for the paramedics

✿ Review: After reading ✿

Use your assessment from hearing the children read to choose any GPCs, words or tricky words that need additional practice.

Read 1: Decoding

- On page 11, point to **off in a flash**. Discuss its meaning (*the paramedics drive off quickly*). Compare "flash" in this context with the meaning of **flashing** on page 8. (*going on and off*)
- Practise reading words that contain adjacent consonants. Encourage the children to sound out and blend the following:

shift	**left**	**crashed**	**must**
still	**Fran**	**straps**	

- Ask the children to pick a page and read a sentence aloud. Say: Can you blend each word in your head before you read it out?

Read 2: Prosody

- Turn to pages 10 and 11, and challenge the children to read the pages as if they were a television broadcaster, explaining what is happening in a documentary.
  - Model reading page 11 expressively. Explain that you have tried to make it sound dramatic. Encourage the children to read page 12 in the same way.
  - Discuss what has happened on page 13, and encourage the children to read Param's words with appropriate expression.

Read 3: Comprehension

- Ask the children to describe any times they have seen an ambulance, and where it was. (Be ready to support any children who have experienced real-life incidents.)
- Discuss the title. Ask: What does it suggest about the paramedics? (e.g. *they have lots of jobs*) Do the children think the paramedics are busy? What makes them think this? (e.g. *they rush from job to job*)
- Encourage the children to think about what it is like to be a paramedic.
  - Ask the children what sort of problems they deal with. (e.g. *helping people who have slipped or fallen, or having a baby*)
  - Discuss what skills and characteristics they need. (e.g. *can drive fast and safely, use a ramp, and put a splint on, stay calm, be patient*)
- Turn to pages 14–15 and ask the children to talk about the paramedics' jobs in their own words using the pictures as prompts.